DANDY and BEANO

FAMOUS FACES
FROM THE COMICS

DESPERATE DAN tucked in to his first cow-pie, the first of many, back in December 1937. The following summer Lord Snooty raised his top hat, and quite a few smiles, in a brand new comic called BEANO.

1951 saw Dennis start menacing, and he hasn't stopped since. Two years later Beryl became a peril and Minnie a minx.

And that was only the beginning. Over the years the Comics Hall of Fame has had to make room for Ginger, The Bash Street Kids, Winker Watson and many others, including much more recent arrivals like Bananaman and Calamity James.

Now, more than half a century after Dan looked at that first cow-pie and reckoned a guy's gotta chew what a guy's gotta chew, here are the legendary names from British comics, together in one book.

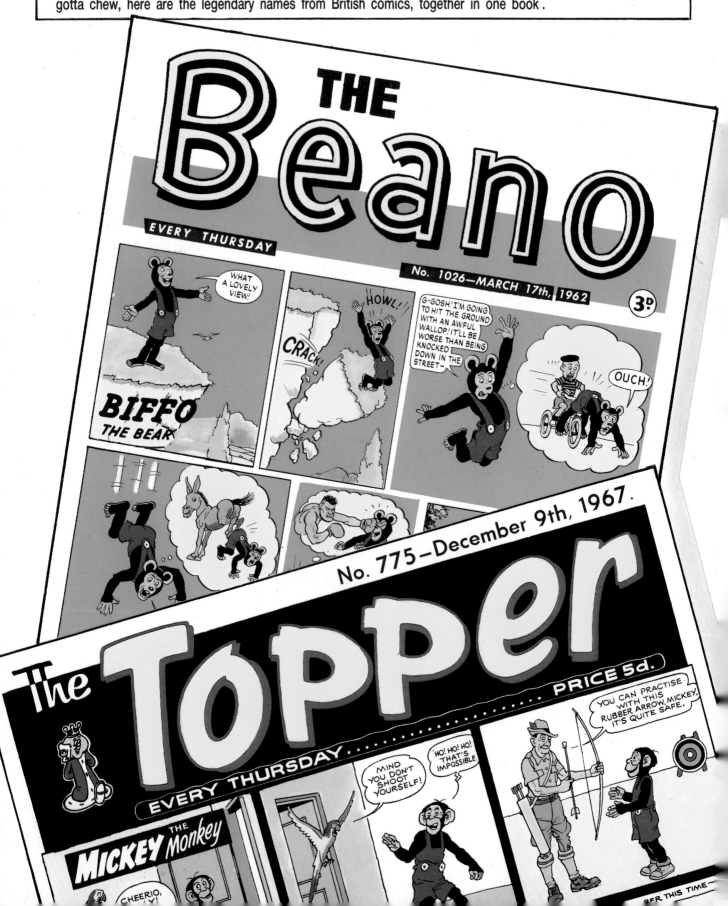

THE COMIC STARS
MODEL FIGURES
COLLECTION

Printed and Published in Great Britain by D. C. Thomson & Co., Ltd., 185 Fleet Street, London.

© **D. C. THOMSON & CO., LTD., 1992**

(Certain stories do not appear as originally published.)

ISBN 0-85116-553-2

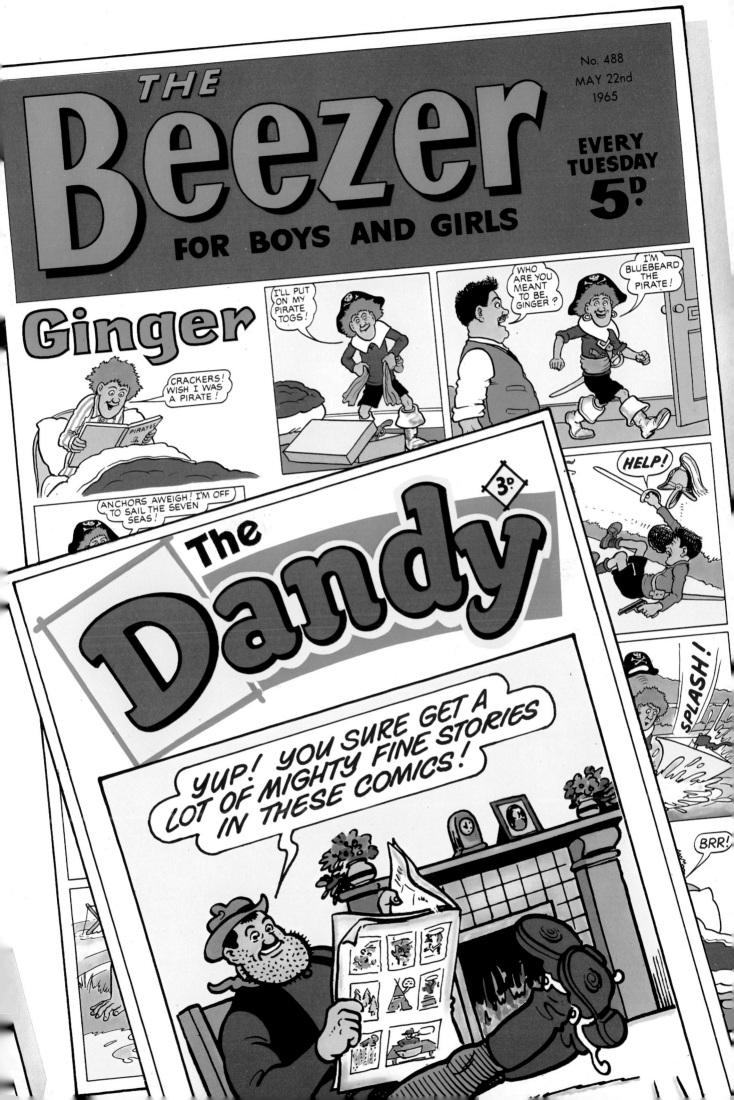

WHAT A DODGER!

Who's the craftiest dodger on the comic scene? No competition! It has to be BEANO'S own Roger The Dodger. No wonder he's good — he's been dodging since 1953.

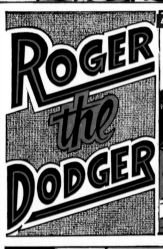

ROGER the DODGER

DURING ART CLASS—
WHAT ON EARTH IS THAT?

IT'S A CHIMNEY-SWEEP STROKING A BLACK CAT IN A COAL CELLAR AT MIDNIGHT!
CHEEK! STAND IN THE CORNER!

IN THE CORNER—
HEH! HEH! JUST AS I PLANNED!

UP PERISCOPE!

AND THIS IS WHAT ROGER IS WATCHING—A FOOTBALL MATCH ACROSS THE ROAD!

HALF-TIME—
I'LL READ MY "BEANO" UNTIL THE SECOND HALF STARTS!

SECOND HALF—
GOAL!

SO IT WAS ALL A DODGE, EH? WELL, YOU CAN GO STRAIGHT INTO THE CORNER IN YOUR NEXT CLASS!
MAYBE THERE'LL BE A WINDOW THERE, TOO!

AND SO—
TEACHER SAYS I'M TO GO STRAIGHT INTO THE CORNER!
GYM

GOOD! YOU'RE JUST IN TIME TO TAKE ON BASHER BRIGGS!
NO! NO! NO!
BOXING CLASS

BIFF! THUD! BAM! BLAM! SPLAT! THUD!

NEXT DAY—
SO! UP TO ROGER'S TRICKS—EH, ALEC?
NO, TEACHER!

THAT'S A DRAWING OF ROGER'S EYES AFTER HIS FIGHT WITH BASHER, SIR!
EXCELLENT! MOST REALISTIC!

ROGER the DODGER

BEANO'S walking disaster area, Calamity James, has done ONE thing right. He's become a comic superstar despite only being on the scene since 1986.

Where there's muck there's laughs! That's something comic fans have always known thanks to grotty geezers like Smiffy in BEEZER and BEANO'S Smudge. But the messiest, dirtiest, scruffiest comic star of them all was DANDY'S Dirty Dick. See for yourself overleaf.

THE BOYS DIRTY DICK

ON MONDAY DICK WAS FAIR OF FACE ~~~

~~~ UNTIL THIS FAT LAD STOOD ON HIS LACE!

ON TUESDAY DICK WAS FULL OF GRACE ~~~

~~~ TILL HE MISSED HIS STEP AND FELL ON HIS FACE!

ON WEDNESDAY HE WAS FULL OF WOE ~~~

~~~ FILTHY DIRTY FROM HEAD TO TOE!

No Contest!

That was the verdict of BEEZER'S readers each week when Pop tried to sort out Dick and Harry. These twins made life difficult for their dad right from the comic's first issue in 1956, and even enjoyed a spell on the front cover. The boys did everything together, a real 'dream team'.

When it came to day-dreaming, SPARKY'S Dreamy Daniel was the champ. Judge for yourself in the story opposite.

DREAMY DANIEL

He lives all alone...in a world of his own!

B

BEEZER BOY

If anyone can claim to be a BEEZER boy it's Ginger. Cover star of the comic's first issue in 1956, he went on to enjoy over 30 years on the comic scene.

IN THEIR OWN WRITE!

Several comic stars have appeared in their own annuals. During the 1950s, Desperate Dan, Dennis The Menace and Beryl The Peril went solo, but Black Bob the DANDY wonderdog beat them all. Bob's first annual was published in time for Christmas 1949, while much more recently, fans of Bananaman and The Bash Street Kids have also enjoyed books featuring their heroes.

If you're one of those readers who thinks you can't get too much of a good thing, then these are the books for you.

KORKY THE CAT is a legend in the comic world. His exploits appeared on DANDY'S front cover from its first issue on 4th December, 1937, until 1984. It was then Korky took up his now-familiar post next to DANDY'S title and was given a page inside the comic.

FAMOUS FACES FROM THE COMICS

CRACK!

In the late 1950s, *CHARLIE THE CHIMP* provided plenty of monkey business in the pages of *DANDY*, but when it came to the great apes, cheeky chimps and mischievous monkeys of the comic world, the undisputed superstar is *MICKEY THE MONKEY. MICKEY* has entertained millions of comic fans since his first appearance on the cover of *TOPPER* issue number one in *1953*.

FAMOUS FACES FROM THE COMICS

THE MENACING MENAGERIE

Dennis knows a thing or two about animals. In fact animals are his pet subject. Today's comic fans are familiar with Gnasher the fang-tastic hound and lots of BEANO readers will remember Rasher the pig's revolting rounds of the farmyard, but back in 1966, before even Gnasher made his first appearance, Dennis introduced a mighty mouse called Denmouse The Mennouse.

CAT and MOUSE . . .

. . . or cat and mice, more accurately. TOPPER'S Scaredy Cat was a late arrival on the comic scene in 1989. He was probably too nervous to turn up any earlier. The Nibblers were making mouse-holes in BEANO back in 1970, but never once bored BEANO'S readers.

SCAREDY CAT

THE CATASTROPHE CAT THAT'S LOST EIGHT LIVES!

Yike! Vicious tortoises! I wish I had a big shell for protection!

RAKE!

Wally!

Funny things happen on this page. Nyarf!

YULCH!

BOOT!

SPLUTCH!

Oh, no! I'm dirty, and you know what that means . . .

. . . bath-time! And us cats hate water!

GURGLE!

BUBBLE!

You can't be too careful.

C-come on, S-Scaredy. Be b-brave and get in. Where's the soap?

SLIP!

NO! I can't get in! Eek! There's the soap!

Oh, dear. This looks like his 9th life gone.

READERS.

BACK FLIP!

CHUNG!

Burble! I had to drink all the bath water to save myself. Where's the nearest plumbers?

Hee! Nice shell, Scaredy.

SPLOOT!

GURGLE!

C

BEARLY A WORD . . .

Biffo The Bear was BEANO'S cover star from 1948 until 1974, but he didn't shout about it. In fact, as you can see here, Biffo was often a bear of few words.

BIFFO
THE BEAR

FREDDY THE FEARLESS FLY

COO! WHAT A LOVELY DISH OF CAKES. I MUST SAMPLE THEM.

OH NO YOU WON'T! I'LL LOCK THEM UP IN THE PANTRY OUT OF YOUR REACH.

THAT'S STOPPED YOUR LITTLE GAME!

THAT'S WHAT HE THINKS —

—THE KEYHOLE IS BIG ENOUGH FOR ME TO GET THROUGH!

HELP! SEPTIMUS SPIDER'S IN HERE TOO!

PHEW! IN FUTURE I'LL LEAVE KEYHOLES TO KEYHOLE KATE!

TOWN 5 MILES

FIGARO

This bandit was the baddest in The West . . . bad at robbing banks, bad at holding up stagecoaches, bad at making his getaway . . . but always good for a laugh, right through the '60s, '70s and '80s in the pages of TOPPER.

DESPERATE DAN

Since DANDY'S first issue in 1937, this Texas tough guy has kept his chin up, which is no easy task when you've a chin as big as Dan's.

DING-DONG BELLE

THIS MARBLES CRAZE IS GETTIN' WORSE AN' WORSE! IF THE MEN ARE LIKE THIS, I WONDER WHAT THE KIDS IN SCHOOL ARE LIKE? I'D BETTER TAKE A LOOK-SEE.

GET OFF OUR MARBLES PITCH, SHERIFF!

CHEAT!

SCHOOL

TUT! TUT! HOW DISTRACTING! THAT NOSEY SHERIFF HAS SLIPPED ON OUR MARBLES, AND SPOILT THE GAME!

WHAT A PITY! WE WERE WORKING THE GAME OUT IN MATHEMATICS TOO!

WELL, BOYS~ UNTIL WE CAN FIX UP THE FINALS IN THE SCHOOL MARBLES CONTEST, WE'LL HAVE A BIT OF GEOGRAPHY.

COO! THERE'S LOTS OF NEW RIVERS!

THOSE ARE CRACKS!

ONE HOUR LATER

HEY, KIDS! DO YOU MIND IF I HAVE A GAME JUST TO PASS THE TIME?

I'LL PUT A STOP TO THIS MARBLES CRAZE!

JOIN IN, SHERIFF!

TWO HOURS LATER

YOU CAN'T SEE BELLE, BUT SHE'S SOMEWHERE BEHIND THAT MOUNTAIN OF MARBLES SHE'S WON, AND STILL WINNING MORE!

THAT WAS MINE~ THAT ONE THERE!

KEEP OFF OR ELSE!

TWO AND A HALF HOURS LATER

SHE'S WON THE LOT! THERE'S NOT ANOTHER MARBLE IN TOWN!

MARBLES

MARBLES

MARBLES

NOW FOR THE STORE-KEEPER!

GENERAL STORE

I RECOGNISED YOU WHEN I BOUGHT MY MARBLES, MISTER STOREMAN~ YOU'RE WANTED FOR STEALING A WAGON TRAIN OF MARBLES AND TOYS FOR THE KIDS OF COWVILLE. GET GOING! I'VE GOT A JOB FOR YOU!

SEVEN HUNDRED AND SIXTY-TWO THOUSAND SIX HUNDRED AND THIRTY FOUR. AND I COUNTED 'EM ONE BY ONE THIS TIME!

THAT'S THREE TIMES YOU'VE GOT IT DIFFERENT. NOW COUNT 'EM AGAIN. WHEN I SEND THESE MARBLES OFF TO COWVILLE, I WANT TO BE SURE THAT THEY'RE ALL THERE.

DESPERATE DAN

DAN IS SOUND ASLEEP. HIS ALARM IS RINGING, BUT HE DOESN'T HEAR IT.

'KATEY AND DANNY ARE SOUND ASLEEP, TOO, ALTHOUGH THEIR ALARM IS ALSO RINGING.

IN FACT, ALL CACTUSVILLE IS ASLEEP—EVEN THE MILKMAN!

—AND THE COCKERELS ARE SNORING IN EVERY HEN-HOUSE.

THE TROUBLE STARTED ON NEW YEAR'S EVE WHEN THE BELL-RINGER WENT TO RING IN THE NEW YEAR—

THE BELL CAME UNSTUCK AT THE FIRST TUG OF THE ROPE AND FELL ON HIM.

DESPERATE DAN WAS CALLED TO LIFT IT OFF.

THEN THE MAYOR HAD A WORD WITH DAN. HOW CAN WE RING IN THE NEW YEAR? LEAVE IT TO ME.

I'LL CARRY THE BELL ROUND THE TOWN AND RING IT MYSELF. OH! WHAT A ROW!

STOP! STOP! YOU'RE DEAFENING US! DAN WON'T STOP. HE CAN'T HEAR US TELLING HIM BECAUSE OF THE DIN. THE BELL'S NOT WORKING NOW. I MUST HAVE CRACKED IT.

OH WELL, I'LL USE IT TO HAVE A DRINK OF GINGER POP TO WELCOME IN THE NEW YEAR.

HAPPY NEW YEAR, EVERYBODY!

DAN GOES TO BED WONDERING WHY EVERYTHING IS SO QUIET ON NEW YEAR'S MORNING.

WHEN DAYLIGHT COMES, CACTUSVILLE SLUMBERS ON, DEAF TO TELEPHONES, CHIMING CLOCKS, CUCKOO CLOCKS, TRAIN WHISTLES, BIRD WHISTLES, DOG BARKS AND COCKCROWS.

WHEN DAN'S ALARM WENT OFF, DAN SLEPT RIGHT ON.

9 a.m.

SUFFERING CATS! LOOK AT THE TIME! MY ALARM COULDN'T HAVE GONE OFF! I SET IT FOR SEVEN.

SAY, I'M SPEAKING, BUT I CAN'T HEAR MYSELF. I MUST HAVE LOST MY VOICE!

OUTSIDE— I KNOW A GOOD CURE FOR THAT—A NEW YEAR SWIM IN THE FROZEN CANAL!

LOOK AT DAN SWIMMING IN THE FROZEN CANAL! IT MAKES MY TEETH CHATTER TO WATCH!

EVERYONE'S TEETH ARE CHATTERING. I CAN SEE THEM, BUT I CAN'T HEAR.

LOVELY! NOW I CAN HEAR MYSELF SPEAKING. THERE'S NOTHING LIKE THIS FOR CURING TROUBLES!

BUT DAN WAS THE ONLY ONE WHO COULD TAKE THIS KIND OF CURE. SO EVERYONE ELSE IN CACTUSVILLE STAYED DEAF FOR A WEEK!

D WATKINS

Readers of BEANO during the 1960s knew that Jonah was the comic star who gave fellow sailors that sinking feeling. There wasn't a ship afloat that stayed afloat once Jonah ventured on board.

INTRODUCING— CORNELIUS B. PROUT, MAKER OF FIVE-HOUR-LONG, HISTORICAL, SPECTACULAR FILMS.

MY NEXT FILM'LL BE SENSATIONAL, FOLKS!

THE NEXT FILM, "BEN HIM", STARS CARY CURTIS, WHO PLAYS THE PART OF A ROMAN GALLEY SLAVE.

A ROMAN GALLEY HAS BEEN BUILT AT GREAT EXPENSE—

—AND FILM EXTRAS HAVE BEEN RECRUITED BY THE HUNDRED.

YOU GUYS ARE GALLEY SLAVES! COLLECT YOUR COSTUMES AND ASSEMBLE AT THE GALLEY.

NOW, THE CHAP WHO CHOSE THESE EXTRAS HAS MADE A GHASTLY MISTAKE—AND, IF YOU STUDY THIS SECTION OF THE QUEUE, YOU'LL SPOT IT!

COSTUME AND MAKE-UP →

STILL UNDETECTED, THE GHASTLY MISTAKE BOARDS THE GALLEY, AND IT SETS SAIL.

OKAY, YOU GUYS. WE START FILMIN' IN FIVE MINUTES!

G-GOSH!—WHEEZE!—I DON'T KNOW WHETHER THIS WAS A GOOD IDEA OR NOT! I THOUGHT I'D HAVE BEEN GIVEN THE PART OF CAP'N O' THIS TUB!

HEE! HEE! POOR SAP!

HEY, YOU! YOU'RE NOT ROWING! WHAT'S THE IDEA, MATE?

NATURALLY I'M NOT ROWING, YOU OAF! **I'M** CARY CURTIS, THE STAR OF THIS FILM! YOU DON'T EXPECT ME TO BLISTER MY HANDS, DO YOU?

LOOK, MATE! I DON'T CARE **WHO** YOU ARE! EITHER YOU GIVE ME A HAND ON THIS OAR OR I'LL GIVE YOU A PUNCH ON THE HOOTER!

WOW!

HELP!—GASP!—GANGWAY!—THERE'S A RAVING CRACKPOT ABOARD!

COME BACK AN' PULL YOUR WEIGHT, YOU SHIRKER!

LEMME OUT!

CARY'S PANIC-STRICKEN PLUNGE THROUGH THE GALLEY CAUSES CONFUSION.

ERK! WHERE'S ME OAR?

AWLK!

HOLD IT! CUT! SOMETHING'S HAPPENED TO THE PORT-SIDE OARSMEN!

BUT THE OARSMEN ON THE STARBOARD SIDE OF THE GALLEY ARE STILL PULLING WITH CLOCKWORK PRECISION—

ONE—OUT! TWO—OUT! THREE—OUT!

—AND AS A RESULT—

G-GOLLY! SHE'S TURNIN' STRAIGHT FOR US!

SHIFT THAT BLITHERIN'—OH!—TOO LATE!

AGH-H! I SAID ALL ALONG WE SHOULD HAVE USED A RUBBER BATTERIN' RAM— HELP!

CRASH!

THE FOOLS! THEY'RE HEADING STRAIGHT FOR THE CLIFFS!

AGH-H!

EVERYBODY OFF, QUICK!

CRUMP!

AND SO—

WHO CARES ABOUT YOUR PERISHIN' PERM? HERE! TAKE THIS AND START CHOPPIN' UP WHAT'S LEFT OF THE GALLEY! YOU'LL SELL FIREWOOD, CARY CURTIS, AND LIKE IT! WE'VE GOT TO CUT OUR LOSSES!

B-BUT!

ARMED FARCES

CORPORAL CLOTT

I'VE GOT A NEW JOB. I'M IN CHARGE OF THE CAMP STORES. IT'S JUST LIKE BEING IN A SHOP.

AH, GOOD MORNING, SERGEANT! CAN I HELP YOU?

STORES

YES—I WANT A PAIR OF SIZE TEN BOOTS!

PHEW! THE SIZE TEN BOOTS ARE ON THE TOP SHELF.

YOU WANT A BOX OF SIX INCH NAILS? WELL, JUST HELP YOURSELF— PULL THE STRING MARKED NAILS!

LATER—

NOW I'LL HAVE NO MORE TROUBLE CLIMBING THIS LADDER. I'VE GOT EVERYTHING THAT'S OUT OF REACH TIED TO A LABELLED STRING! BRAINY, EH?

NAILS

BOOTS

EEK! THE COLONEL!

YOU'RE IN LUCK, SIR! WE HAVE A SET OF FALSE TEETH IN STORE! TRY THEM FOR SIZE!

GRRR! I DIDN'T COME FOR FALSE TEETH! I WANT STRING!

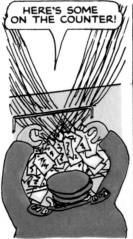

HERE'S SOME ON THE COUNTER!

LOOK WHAT YOU'VE DONE, SIR—PULLED ALL THE STORES DOWN!

During the 1970s, readers of **THE SPARKY** reckoned this World War I flier was ace!

BARON VON REICHS-PUDDING— YOU VILL FLY DER SUPERDUPER-GENERAL FLABBERTUM TO DER H.Q.! HE IS MAKING DER PLAN FOR WINNING DER WAR!

PROUD TO BE OF ASSISTANCE, MINE SUPERDUPER-GENERAL!

GOOT! ZEN KINDLY ASSIST ME INTO MINE SEAT!

DER GASP!

GET DER MOVE ON, VON REICHS-PUDDING!

VOT A WEIGHT! MINE POOR AEROPLANE!

CREAK!

ACHTUNG! YOU ARE TOO HEFFY, MINE SUPERDUPER-GENERAL! WE HAFF NOT LIFT-OFF!

VOT? RUBBISH! IT IS DER STINKENROTTEN PLANE VOT ISS AT FAULT!

CRASH!

DER LATER—

AN EXCELLENT IDEA OF MINE TO GIVE US DER START MIT DER BALLOON, ISS IT NOT?

JUST GET ON MIT IT, DUMBSKULL!

VE HAFF LIFT-OFF! I CAN NOW RELEASE DER BALLOON!

GOOT!

!!

VE MUST LOSE WEIGHT! PLEASE THROW OUT YOUR MEDALS!

VOT? ACH! VERY WELL———

Even BEEZER readers with long memories won't recall seeing this colonel in uniform.

He has the distinction of being retired by the time his career began . . . his career as a comic superstar that is!

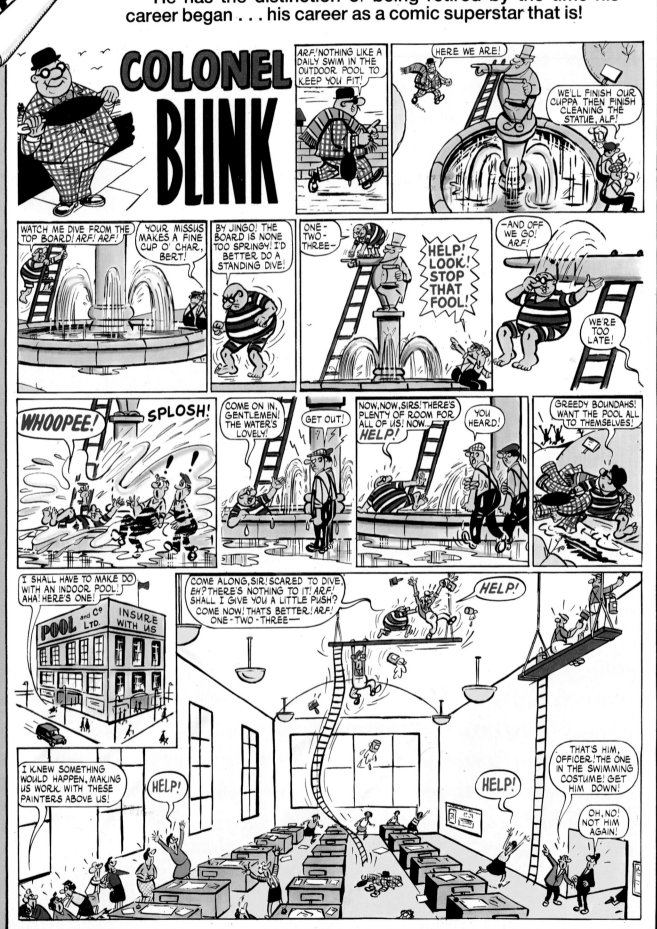

PUTTING DENNIS IN THE SHADE

There's only one way to put Britain's number one menace in the shade and that's by making a Dennis The Menace table lamp. And a lamp isn't the only item to have featured that famous face. Dennis, and a select band of his comic cronies, have appeared on everything from plates and rugs to clocks and mugs. A selection of mirth-making merchandise appears overleaf.

BIG BABY, BIG STAR!

Baby Crockett may look like a youngster but he was 'big' in BEEZER back in the 1950s, while young Ivy on the opposite page didn't get a chance to be terrible in BEANO until 1985.

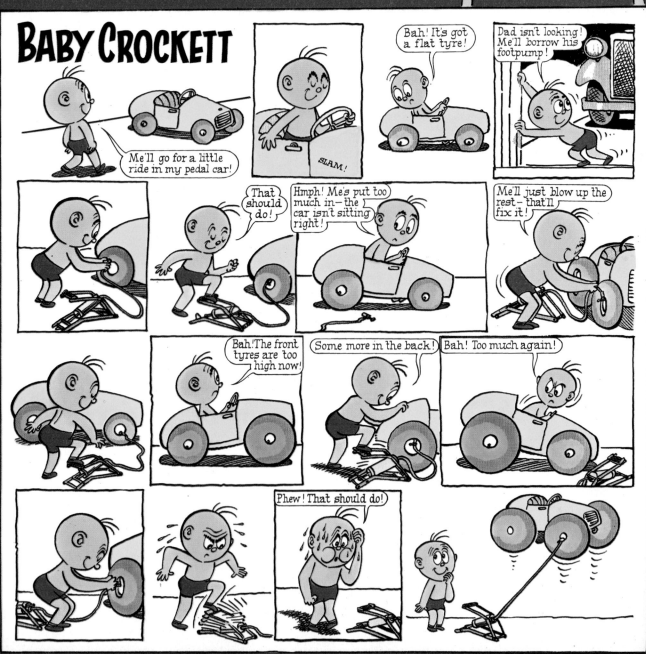

Babyface Finlayson became BEANO'S cutest bandit in 1972. The Ali's Baba saga opposite appeared in SPARKY three years later.

MICRO QUIPS

Cuddles and Dimples

ME GOT PIMPLE ON NOSE.

ME GOT SPOT ON ME —

ALL LITTLE BOYS HAVE PIMPLES.

SO I USE TALC!

WE LIKE BUBBLES!

UBBLE! N-NO! DON'T! N-O-O-O!

POOR DAD! CLEAN AS A BABY

THAT'LL DO, DEAR.

I'LL HANDLE THE BOYS.

NOW, LITTLE DARLINGS, YOU'LL BATH, POWDER, AND EAT —

AMAZING!

OH, I DON'T THINK SO. US MUMMIES HAVE A WAY WITH KIDS.

FAMOUS CARS
AND THEIR BADGES

IT'S A FACT! DURING THE 1950s AND INTO THE '60s TOPPER MIXED FACTS WITH THE FUNNIES. EACH WEEK THE COMIC CARRIED BEAUTIFULLY ILLUSTRATED FEATURES ON ANYTHING FROM MOTHS TO MOTORING.

DE SOTO "Fireflite"
(AMERICAN)
Top speed about
110 miles per hour.

MERCEDES-BENZ "300 SL"
(GERMAN)
Top speed about
150 miles per hour.

SUNBEAM "Rapier"
(BRITISH)
Top speed about
90 miles per hour.

SUNBEAM RAPIER

ROVER "3-LITRE"
(BRITISH)
Top speed about
100 miles per hour

VOLVO "Amazon S"
(SWEDISH)
Top speed about
90 miles per hour.

VOLVO

PORSCHE "Convertible D"
(GERMAN)
Top speed about
100 miles per hour.

FORD "Thunderbird"
(AMERICAN)
Top speed about
115 miles per hour.

FORD

Austin

ALL ABOUT TREES

LEAVES

TULIP TREE

FLOWER

The TULIP TREE gets its name from its tulip-like flowers. It is a tall tree, sometimes growing to a height of 100 feet. Its smooth, fine-grained timber is ideal for panelling.

SUMMER

WINTER

LOCUST TREE

FLOWERS

LEAVES

SUMMER

SUMMER

FINE FEATHERS
SOME OF THE WORLD'S MOST BEAUTIFUL BIRDS

RED-FRONTED TINKER-BIRD
Eritrea, Abyssinia and
British Somaliland.

SMALL SUNBIRD
Ceylon and
South-West India

NUBIAN WOODPECKER
Eastern Belgian Congo to Eritrea,
Abyssinia, British Somaliland
and Tanganyika.

NATURE PARADE

The ARABIAN SAND CAT, also found in the Sahara Desert, parts of North Africa and South Russia, lives in a hole in the sand. It comes out only at night to hunt for food.

The SPIDER FLOWER, of South ... jungles, gets its name from its rese... to the insect of the same nar...

...EDGE.
...res up

The GUILLEMOT is a common bird on some parts of the British coast. Guillemot eggs are of a very unusual shape, so sharply tapered that they will not easily roll off the cliff ledges on which they are laid.

...of the Gibbons, the SIAMANG, is only three feet ...s an arm span of almost six feet. It has an unusual ...which can be blown up like a balloon, probably to ...nemies. It lives in the forests of Sumatra and the Malay Peninsula.

...s name, the FIREFLY is really a ...s luminous and shines quite ...rightly in the dark.

BEAUTIFUL BUTTERFLIES

ZEBRA SWALLOWTAIL
Throughout Eastern U.S.A.

LARGE SALMON ARAB
North-West and Central India

COMMON GRASS YELLOW
North Australia

COMMON IMPERIAL
Ceylon, India and Burma

CRIMSON ROSE
Bengal and Southern India

GAUDY COMMODOR
Central Africa.

...G BUTTERFLY
...and Sumatra.

LONG TAILED SKIPPER
Tropical America and as far North as New York.

ALIVE, ALIVE-O!
FISH OF BRITAIN'S LAKES AND RIVERS

BREAM

CHAR

POWAN

GRAYLING

LAMPREY

TENCH

PIKE

Meet the guys who put the rootin' tootin' feudin' 'n' shootin' into BEEZER.

Meet the guys who have provided fighting, feuding and fun in DANDY since 1975.

THE JOCKS and the GEORDIES

ARE YOU READY, JOCKS? WE'VE ALL SEEN OUR WRESTLING HERO, THE MASHER, ON TELEVISION. LET'S TRY OUT SOME OF HIS HOLDS.

THEN USE THEM ON THE GEORDIES. HO-HO!

THERE'S THE BELL FOR THE START OF ROUND ONE.

SNIGGER! THE JOCKS ARE SO BUSY, THEY HAVEN'T SPOTTED US. AND LOOK! THEY'RE USING A RUNNING NOOSE ROUND THEIR RING.

GAAH!

GASP!

RIGHT, LADS! PULL! HO-HO! GOT THE LOT!

EEK! AMBUSHED!

OOYAH!

PULL!

OUCH!

THIS IS THE KIND OF PUNCH-UP I ENJOY!

OOF!

AARGH!

LET'S GO, LADS! THE JOCKS ARE LIKE THE MASHER— THEY'RE HOPELESS!

WE SUPPORT THE MAULER!

LATER—

SNARL! FOLLOW ME, JOCKS! WE'LL TEACH THOSE MAULER FANS.

NO SIGNS OF THE JOCKS, BUT WE MUST WATCH OUT FOR AN AMBUSH, LADS!

HEE-HEE! I'VE FIXED THE BELL ON THE OTHER SIDE OF THE WALL. AND WHEN I PULL ON THIS ROPE—

—THE BELL WILL RING!

AHA! SOUNDS LIKE A FIGHT BELL. THE JOCKS MUST BE OVER THE WALL.

DING!

WE'LL SNEAK OVER AND DROP IN ON THEM— HUH?

OH, NO, YOU WON'T!

COME BACK! GOT YOU!

WAAH! WE'VE BEEN TRICKED!

THEY'RE BANANAS

No wonder they call themselves The Banana Bunch — most of their crazy antics are completely bananas! When BEEZER was launched in 1956 these guys were in the first issue. This is the only Banana Bunch in history that's still fresh after 36 years.

MEET THE MINX

SUGAR and SPICE

MINNIE THE MINX is second only to you-know-who when it comes to menacing and mayhem in the pages of BEANO. Her Dad reckons that trouble is her middle name but Minnie says it's 'The'. One thing that's sure is that Minnie's been around since 1953. And if you think she's grown wilder over the years look at these early stories and think again!

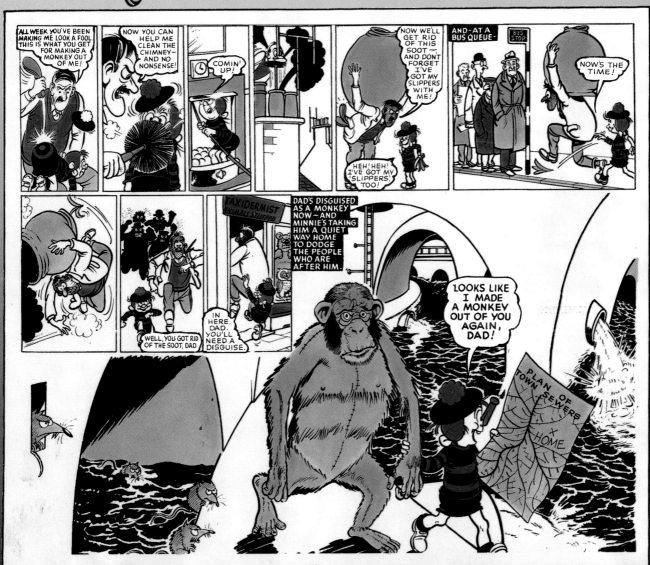

PANSY POTTER
THE STRONGMAN'S DAUGHTER

Pansy Potter didn't only have strength, she had staying power too! From the pages of BEANO'S earliest issues in the 1930's to SPARKY during the 1970's, Pansy's mighty muscles were in evidence.

Another girl who's stayed around is Keyhole Kate. DANDY readers could spy Kate spying from 1937 through to 1955. Kate then popped up to peep in SPARKY during the '60's and '70's before heading home to DANDY in 1989.

KEYHOLE KATE

AND HOW DO YOU LIKE
MY BERYLLIANT PICCIES?

SUGAR and SPICE

1953 was a good year for girls! Minnie The Minx wasn't the only comic star to make her début then. Beryl The Peril appeared for the first time in '53, in a brand new comic called THE TOPPER.

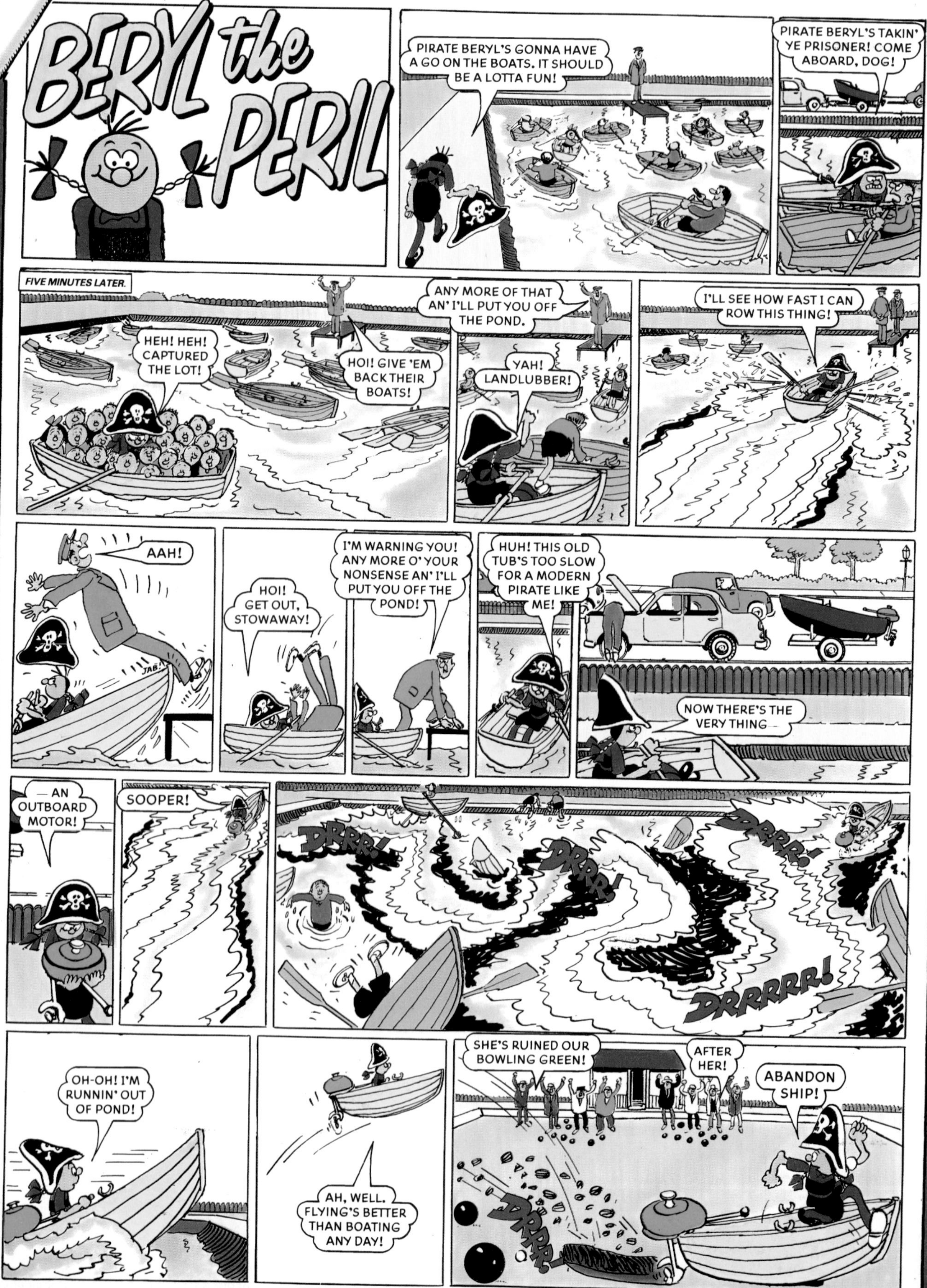

FRED THE FLOP — Fred's life of crime began in the early 1970s in the pages of BUZZ, before he broke into the big time with a regular spot in TOPPER.

THE BADD LADS — Knuck, Fingers and Boss were BEEZER'S bungling baddies. If you need proof that crime doesn't pay here's the evidence.

SEND FOR KELLY — Neither cop nor robber, Nick Kelly was a special agent who divided his time in TOPPER between catching crooks and sniffing out spies.

L. CARS — Cedric and Frederic were a couple of catastrophic cops. Their crime-fighting antics appeared in SPARKY and their inspector reckoned they couldn't catch a cold.

ALI HA HA — Ali's dad was a cop in Baghdad, and his son's attempts to help drove Ali's dad mad! This feast of eastern laughter took place in DANDY in the 1960s.

CRIMINAL RECORDS

FRED the FLOP

CRIME TIME

The Badd Lads have been up to no good since BEEZER'S early years, a real long-running story. And running is what these bungling baddies usually end up doing.

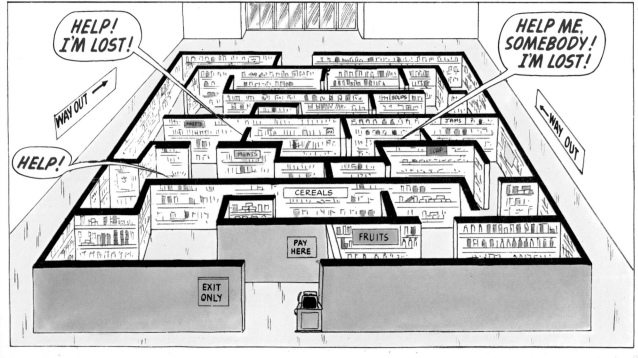

SEND FOR Kelly

and HIS ASSISTANT, CEDRIC.

In an effort to cripple the "Dirty Trick", the old-time pirate ship of Cap'n Blackbeard, Nick Kelly and Cedric disguised themselves as pirates and joined Blackbeard's crew. But now the pirates have discovered who their new recruits really are — so our special agents are in big TROUBLE!

SLAP THE SWABS IN IRONS! WE'LL HAVE SOME SPORT MAKIN' 'EM WALK THE PLANK WHEN WE'RE WELL OUT AT SEA.

HEH—HA—HAR—RR! AYE—AYE, CAP'N BLACKBEARD.

I'M NOT TOO HAPPY ABOUT THIS PLANK-WALKING LARK, MR KELLY — NOT WITH ALL THOSE SHARKS AROUND.

I'M NOT TOO KEEN ABOUT IT MYSELF! HAVE YOU ANY SMART IDEAS?

MEANWHILE, UP CRUISES DOPEY DICK, THE STUPIDEST WHALE IN THE WORLD, WHO IS TRYING TO FIND HIS WAY BACK TO ANTARCTIC WATERS.....

LOOK, CEDRIC! IT'S THAT WHALE AGAIN!

HMPH! NO SNOW ON THAT ISLAND I JUST PASSED. I'M STILL FAR FROM HOME.

I HAVE AN IDEA THAT MIGHT WORK — IF ONLY I CAN SCORE A HIT WHEN I TOSS OUT THIS GUN RAMMER!

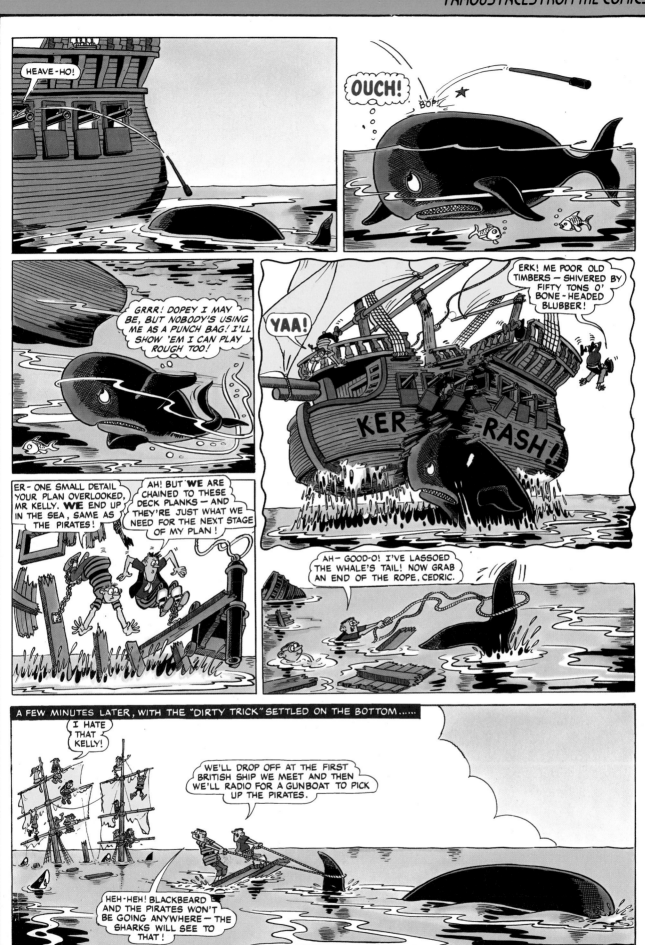

Readers who are too young to remember what fashions were like in 1975 can find out now and 'cop' a few laughs while they're at it.

P.C. CEDRIC

P.C. FREDERIC

THE INSPECTOR

⌐L ⊃ARS ON PARADE!

IT'S MONDAY MORNING!

THIS IS THE INSPECTOR SPEAKING... ALL & CARS MEN WILL GET ON PARADE IMMEDIATELY — IF NOT SOONER! HURRY UP! COME ON! LET'S BE HAVING YOU!

A PARADE — FIRST THING IN THE MORNING,

OH, HE JUST DOESN'T CARE, CEDRIC!

YOU MIGHT PERHAPS BE WONDERING WHY WE ARE HAVING A PARADE TODAY. WELL, THE CHIEF CONSTABLE WILL BE HAVING A PUBLIC INSPECTION OF POLICE OFFICERS AT THE END OF THIS WEEK — AND I WANT YOU ALL PERFECT — SMART, TIDY AND **PROPERLY DRESSED!**

AS FOR YOU . . .

ME, SIR — WHAT'S WRONG WITH ME?

TAKE OFF THOSE SLIPPERS AT ONCE, MAN!

AW, THESE, SIR? WELL, MY CORNS HAVE BEEN A BIT SORE, SIR!

TUESDAY —

SHOULDERS BACK, CHESTS OUT, STOMACHS IN . . . NOW LET'S SEE. I HOPE YOU'RE ALL **PROPERLY DRESSED!**

AND, WHAT MAY I ASK, DO YOU CALL **THIS?**

A TIE, SIR!

BUT IT'S NOT A **POLICE** TIE, IS IT? **GRRR!** DON'T LET THIS HAPPEN AGAIN!

S-S-SIR!

WEDNESDAY —

HELLO, HELLO, HELLO! WHAT'S ALL THIS HERE THEN?

TSK!

ALI HA-HA and the 40 THIEVES

HI, FOLKS! I'VE RECEIVED A SENSIBLE LETTER FROM A LAD CALLED GUFFY GRIPEWATER, OF GRIMSBY! HE SUGGESTS THAT I BUY ALI A PET TO KEEP HIM OCCUPIED, WHILE I GET ON WITH CATCHING THE FORTY THIEVES!

CONGRATULATIONS, GUFFY! I'VE TAKEN YOUR ADVICE AND BOUGHT ALI A PET MOUSE. I'LL GIVE IT TO HIM WHEN HE COMES IN!

SQUEAK

MEANWHILE DAD IS BEING FORESTALLED BY THE LOCAL CIRCUS BOSS —

WILF

THANKS FOR OFFERING TO TAKE WILFRED, ALI. A FEW DAYS REST AND QUIET WILL DO HIM GOOD.

THINK NOTHIN' OF IT!

NOW, HERE'S AN INTERESTING FACT: ONE TINY MOUSE CAN STRIKE TERROR INTO THE HEART OF A FIVE TON BULL ELEPHANT.

AND AS WILFRED HAPPENS TO BE EXACTLY THAT, TERRIBLE THINGS HAPPEN WHEN ALI ARRIVES AT THE COP-SHOP!

AGHH! A HORRIBLE MOUSE!

Y-YES, DAD!

ERK! GET THAT BRUTE OUTA HERE!

SQUEAK

AFTER A QUICK GETAWAY

BANK OF BAGHD

WELL! YOU FAIRLY HASHED UP MY DAD, WILF! NOW WE GOTTA GET BACK IN HIS GOOD BOOKS, AND—! GOSH! MUSTAPHA PHAG AND HIS THIEVES! NOW'S OUR CHANCE.

SMASH DOWN ZE DOORS, LADS!

BAM

FILL UP, WILF! THOSE THIEVES ARE GONNA GET IN THERE SOONER THAN THEY EXPECT!

WHOOSH

HORSE TROUGH

AR-R-RGH! SUFFERIN' SULTANS! ZE MONSOON SEASON'S STARTED EARLY!

LET 'EM HAVE IT, WILF!

WOW!

SLUR-R-R-P!

5 MINUTES LATER

GR-R-R! SO THERE YOU ARE, YOU PEST!

D-DON'T SHOOT, DAD! I'VE CAPTURED THE 40 THIEVES! WILF'S GOT 'EM PINNED IN THE BANK, WITH HIS REAR END!

HONEST INJUN?

YES!

GOOD FOR YOU, SON! I FORGIVE YOU FOR THAT SHAMBLES! WHAT'S MORE, I'VE RECAPTURED YOUR LITTLE PET MOUSE, AND—

SQUEAK

SCREECH!

THIS ISN'T A WHOLE HERD OF ELEPHANTS STAMPEDING! IT'S JUST WILFRED — GONE STARK, RAVIN' BONKERS!

HELP!

AGH-H! CALL IT OFF!

ONE PULVERIZED POLICE SERGEANT LATER

SHRIEK!!

KEEP IT UP WILF! IF WE CAN GET OVER THAT BORDER INTO SYRIA, HE CAN'T TOUCH US!

SYRIA

WHILE BACK IN BAGHDAD —

IT'S NO USE RUNNING THIS WAY, SARGE! HE WENT THAT WAY TOWARDS SYRIA! I SAW HIM

SNARL!

SYRIA

I AIN'T AFTER ALI! I'M GOIN' TO THE AIRPORT TO GET A TICKET TO ENGLAND! —AN' WHEN I GET MY PERISHIN' HANDS ON THAT LITTLE NIT, GUFFY GRIPEWATER OF GRIMSBY— I'LL PULVERIZE THE PERISHER!

GUFFY GRIPEWATER IS PERHAPS FICTITIOUS. HOWEVER, SHOULD THERE BE A BOY WITH THIS NAME, HE HAS OUR DEEPEST SYMPATHY. ANYONE WITH A NAME LIKE THAT DESERVES SYMPATHY. ALSO, IN THE EVENT OF SUCH A COINCIDENCE, THE EDITOR AND STAFF OF THE DANDY ACKNOWLEDGE NO RESPONSIBILITY SHOULD THE POOR BLIGHTER BE BASHED ON THE BONCE IN GRIMSBY NEXT WEEK, BY A TURKISH TWERP BRANDISHING A WHOPPING GREAT CLUB.

WEIRD and WONDERFUL

Some of the comic scene's big names are only a few inches high, but despite their size, guys like Tiny Tim and Splodge can be quite a handful, and they aren't the only way-out characters around. The comics have always been packed with stories about wizards who can't spell and superheroes who are not particularly super and far from heroic. Now's your chance to meet all those weird and wonderful comic stars in one book . . . MAGIC!

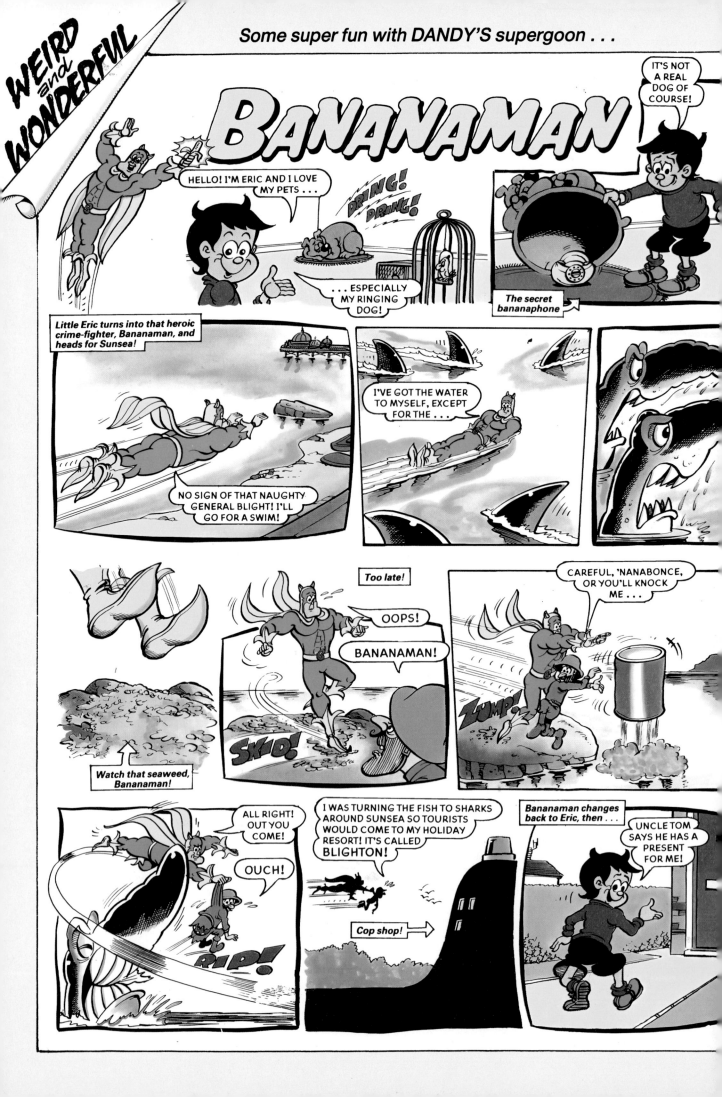

ADRIAN THE BARBARIAN

Dinner —

DON'T PLAY WITH YOUR FOOD, ADRIAN!

OOPS! MY SAUSAGE TWITCHED!

GASP! IT'S ALIVE!

I'M STARVING!

IT'S GROWING! THIS IS CRAZY!

THAT'S BETTER — LET'S PLAY!

ER — OK!

HIDE AND SEEK! I'LL HIDE!

TASTY AROMA!

HERE I COME, READY OR NOT!

I KNOW WHERE HE IS!

GOT YOU! THAT WAS MORE LIKE HIDE AND SNIFF!

SAUSAGE SMELL

RUGBY NOW!

GO GET HIM!

Here's a golden opportunity to meet a comic star with a brass neck. In fact he has a brass head and a brass body too. But a brass neck doesn't always make you unpopular. Brassneck has been a golden boy with DANDY readers since 1964.

BRASSNECK

FUNNY SPELLS AHEAD!

That was the forecast for TOPPER readers during the '50s, '60s and '70s when they turned to stories featuring madcap magician Big Fat Boko. TOPPER was also home to Tiny Tim, a comic star who was so small he could have gone mountaineering on Boko's lunch.

Sam Silkworm does a roaring trade—with the smallest parachutes ever made!

SKOOL ROOLZ

REPORT

WINKER WATSON: Nicknamed the 'Wily Wangler', Winker has been Greytowers School's trickiest pupil since his DANDY debut in 1961. Don't take our word for it, ask Winker's grumpy teacher, Mr Creep.

OLD MA MURPHY: This strong-arm school ma'rm's teaching was strict, but during the 1940s DANDY readers reckoned it was strictly for laughs.

THE BASH STREET KIDS: This classroom classic was called 'When The Bell Rings' when the story first appeared in BEANO back in 1954. Since then the Bash Street pupils' antics have made their school a household name.

GREEDY PIGG: If you think teachers always show a good example, think again! With his grub-grabbing and food-filching, this master's behaviour was worse than any of his pupils. Still, DANDY readers must have approved. From his first appearance in 1965 Greedy Pigg was around for almost 20 Years.

OLD MA MURPHY
THE STRONG-ARM SCHOOL-MA'RM

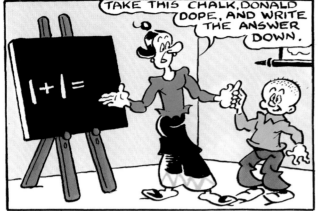

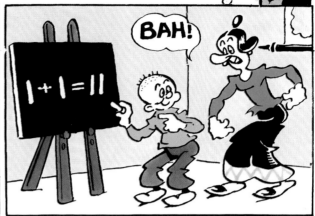

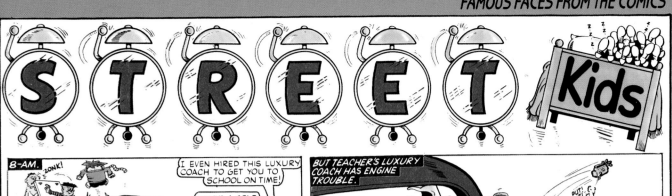

WINKER WATSON

"HERE'S MUD IN YOUR EYE, WINKER! HEE-HEE!"

SCHOOL photographs were to be taken at Greytowers School today. But Winker Watson and his pals were in no fit state to be snapped. They were muddy from top to toe — perhaps because they didn't fancy brushing their hair for the photographer!

NOTICES
THE PHOTOGRAPHER WILL BE IN ATTENDANCE TODAY FOR SCHOOL PHOTOGRAPHS.
MASTERS AT 2. P.M.
PUPILS AT 2.15. P.M.

"COME AND MEET MY THIRD FORMERS, MR. BROMIDE ..."

"DELIGHTED, MR. CREEP."

"WHAT A STATE! GO AND GET DRESSED UP!"

"YES, SIR!"

Winker had never once been caned. And Creepy didn't threaten to cane him now! He just gave an order.

"THIS WAY, CHAPS! CREEPY SAID TO DRESS UP — WE MUST OBEY!"

STORE ROOM
SCHOOL DRAMATIC SOCIETY
OUT of BOUNDS

Winker wasn't called the school's wiliest wangler for nothing. He was up to something!

"OKAY, MR. CREEP SIR?"

"YOU LITTLE MONKEYS! — GO AND GET DRESSED UP PROPERLY!"

Yes. Winker had been up to something dramatic. The boys reappeared in fancy dress, led by Cap'n Winker Watson!

Back in the Store Room—

Winker was up to something else.

"THIS ISN'T GOING TO BE EASY, BOYS — WE'LL HAVE TO CUT UP ALL THIS OLD FUR ...."

"TUT-TUT! WHERE ARE THOSE BOYS? — I CAN HEAR THEM CHATTERING ..."

Mr Creep came striding along to see what monkey tricks were going on ...

What a shock Creepy got. The little monkeys were really up to monkey tricks, dressed in monkey outfits.

Creepy gave the boys a dressing-down again.

"YOU IMPUDENT WRETCHES! I WANT YOU IN YOUR UNIFORMS — AND AS SMART AS GUARDS ON PARADE!"

"YESSIR!"

READY, CHAPS? — THIS SHOULD PLEASE CREEPY! HEE-HEE! QUICK MARCH!

Once more the boys were ready to leave their dressing-room.

WATSON, COME HERE!

HUP! ONE, TWO...

And this time the boys were in uniform — but not school uniform! Wily Winker and his guardsmen had carried out Creepy's order to the letter! But still Creepy wasn't satisfied!

THIS IS YOUR DOING, BOY! SIX OF THE BEST WILL KNOCK THAT GRIN OFF YOUR FACE....

It looked as if Winker's no-caning record would go. But the young guardsman drew his sword.

CHOP!

—And look what he did with it! What a nerve! Just then the Head came on the scene.

Poor Creepy. His actions had been misunderstood.

REALLY, MR. CREEP! THIS IS NO TIME TO BE PLAYING AT SOLDIERS! WATSON AND THE REST OF YOU BOYS GO AND GET DRESSED CORRECTLY!

YESSIR! COME ON, CHAPS!

LATER~~

I'M GOING TO GET EVEN WITH OLD CREEPY!

I'LL TAKE THE TEACHERS FIRST, MR. CREEP.

Winker was planning yet another trick.

....I'LL SWITCH OLD BROMIDE'S CAMERA FOR THIS TRICK ONE....

The teachers were due for a shocking exposure.

..... ON SECOND THOUGHTS, MR. CREEP, I'LL DO THE BOYS FIRST AND GET THEM OUT OF THE WAY!

RIGHT! — LINE UP BOYS!

But it was Winker who got the shock when a sudden change of plan was made. He and his pals were to be taken first.

NOT YOU, WATSON, YOU SCRUFFY LITTLE WRETCH!

HOLD IT, BOYS...

However, Winker was banned from the class photo. What a relief to him!

PHEW! THANKS, MR. CREEP, SIR!

Winker's classmates put on their best smiles for the photograph. But all smiles disappeared when out of the camera shot a jet of black ink!

I DON'T THINK WE NEED PUNISH THE CULPRIT, HEADMASTER, — THAT'LL BE DONE FOR US!

....B-BUT, LISTEN, CHAPS....

Winker's wangle had boomeranged! Now he was being chased by his own classmates. And if he's caught what a pretty picture he'll be!

TWO'S COMPANY

Two's company . . . three's a crowd, the old saying tells us, but on the comic scene *Two* can be a crowd. Another old saying claims it takes two to make an argument but on the following pages you'll discover it takes two to make us laugh.

In DANDY between 1963 and '67, Big Head, the brainy one, had a lot to put up with from Thick Head the . . . er, not-so-brainy one . . .

Big Head and Thick Head

... And when brain and brawn bowed out in 1967, another duelling duo took their place. Step forward . . .

PUSS an' BOOTS

The late 1960s was the hippie era, the time of peace and love, but it was also then that a new double act appeared on the comic scene. *Puss An' Boots* had no time for peace and love, but they did love tearing each other to pieces. This duelling duo fought like cat and dog in the pages of SPARKY.

WE ARE HAPPY TO ANNOUNCE . . .

The adverts on these two pages alerted comic fans to the arrival of brand new titles at their local newsagent's. Of course, when young readers saw the names DANDY, BEANO, BEEZER and TOPPER for the first time, they'd no way of knowing that those publications were destined to become legends of the British comic scene.

OLDIES BUT GOLDIES

A couple of comic stars who are 'oldies' in more ways than one are Desert Island Dick and Grandpa. They're both adults, in fact Grandpa is a senior citizen, as you'll discover when you read the story opposite, and they're both veterans of the comic scene. Desert Island Dick spent many lonely years in TOPPER while Grandpa's geriatric japes appeared in BEANO.

DESERT ISLAND DICK

HO! HUM! ANOTHER DAY DAWNS!

OHO! A CHAIR'S BEEN WASHED ASHORE!

A PERFECT FIT!

SUCH COMFORT! YAWN!

WHAT'S THIS?

EXCUSE ME, BUD—BUT YOU'RE SITTING IN MY CHAIR!

OUT!

THE FIRST MAN TO ROW ROUND THE WORLD IN AN ARMCHAIR—THAT'S MY AMBITION!

WHAT A ROTTEN ISLAND THIS IS, OLLY.

NOT EVEN A COUPLE OF CHAIRS TO SIT ON...

MEANWHILE—

WE'RE RUNNING SHORT OF FUEL. WE'LL HAVE TO CHUCK OUT THE PASSENGER SEATS TO LIGHTEN THE AIRCRAFT. TELL THE STEWARDESS...

SO...

ATTENTION, EVERYONE—DON'T BE ALARMED, BUT HERE'S WHAT I WANT YOU TO DO...

THAT'S THE LOT!

OH, THIS ROTTEN ISLAND! CAN'T MOVE FOR CHAIRS!

HO! HO! LISTEN TO HIM. HE'S NEVER SATISFIED. HO! HO!

GRANDPA

YIPPEE! PENSION DAY TODAY!

NO TOAST AN' MARGE' FOR ME, DAD, I'M IN THE MONEY!

HEH-HEH! ALWAYS GIVE WAY TO YOUR ELDERS IN THE POST OFFICE.

PENSIONS HERE

GOT IT! NOW I'M OFF FOR SWEETS. COMING, CHAPS?

OFFICE

YOU BET!

BUT NEWS SPREADS QUICKLY— FALL-IN, CHAPS, GRANDPA'S TREATING US TO SWEETS.

TEE-TUM TI-TEE!

BOY! I MUST BE IN ON THIS.

—AND AT THE SHOP—

HE WANTS SIX BAGS OF BULL'S-EYES, THREE BAGS OF ANISEED BALLS, A DOZEN ICED-LOLLIES AND TWO DOZEN GOB-STOPPERS!

YUM-YUM!

BOY! YUM! SMASHIN'! LUVLY! GOOD OLD GRANDPA!

SWE

SWEETS &

LOOK AT THAT! TWO BOB CHANGE!

5 MINUTES LATER—

HEY, LOOK JOE! HERE'S GRANDPA, HE USED TO BE THE FITTEST BOY IN CLASS. 'BET HE CAN'T WALK ON HIS HANDS NOW—LIKE HE USED TO!

BAH!

HI, GRANDPA! REMEMBER US? JOE BLOGGS AND BILL BRIGGS—YOUR OLD SCHOOL MATES. WE WERE JUST SAYING—BET YOU CAN'T WALK ON YOUR HANDS ANY MORE?

OH, NO?

WE'RE NOT ALL DODDERIN' OLD FOSSILS, YOU KNOW. HOW'S THIS?

RIGHT, BILL! —GRAB 'EM!

HUP

CHINK

THANKS, PAL.—THAT'S US SQUARE FOR THE TWO BOB YOU BORROWED FROM US TO BUY ACID-DROPS IN 1886!

AT LAST! —AFTER 70 YEARS!

EMPTY

NEXT PENSION DAY—

NO-IT ISN'T A FOREIGN SPY—

POST OFFICE

—IT'S GRANDPA, GOING TO DRAW HIS PENSION — IN DISGUISE!

One glance at the wartime adventure opposite, and you'll know that Lord Snooty has been a comic star for a long time. In fact, Snooty appeared in ***BEANO'S*** first issue 'way back in 1938.

Comic fans must have a taste for gluttons if Hungry Horace is anything to go by. He appeared in DANDY from issue number one before moving on to SPARKY and then TOPPER.

But when it comes to moving, no-one moves faster than BEANO'S Billy Whizz. See for yourself on the opposite page.

Hungry Horace

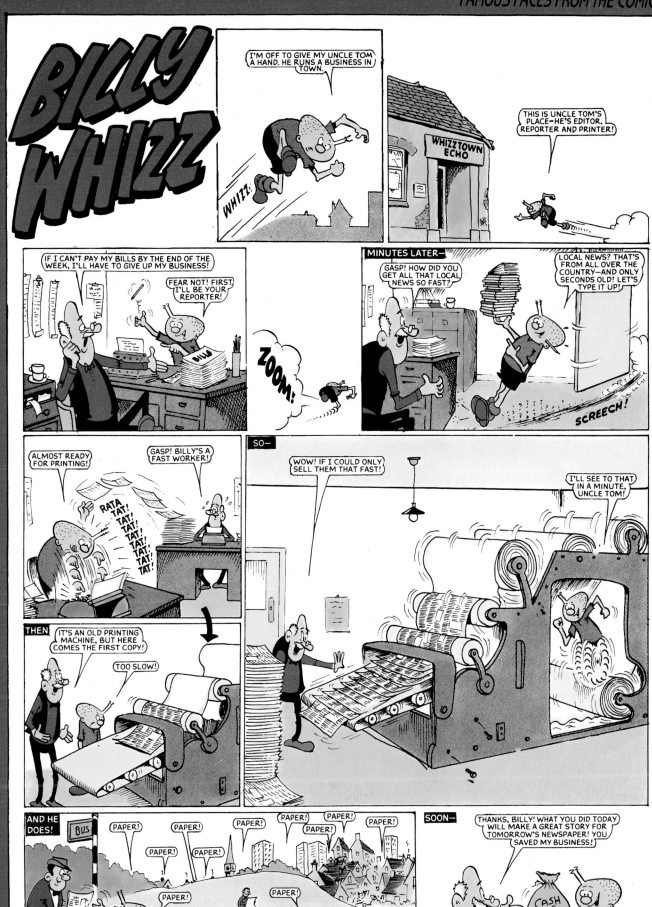

HE'S
Tricky

TOPPER'S Tricky Dicky has been around since 1976 with his jokes, jests, tricks and gags. The lad himself hasn't always come off best, but that's not something you could say about Dicky's fans.

PODGE

NEVER HEARD OF HIM!

Mention the name 'Podge' to today's young comic fans and that's what they'll probably say, but during the 1940s Podge was big in the comic world (and around the waistline). Podge appeared in DANDY'S first issue back in 1937 and stayed around for seven years.

A SHORT HISTORY OF DENNIS

1951 — First appearance in BEANO. Black and white only and half a page.

1953 — Expanded to a full page and two colours (red and black).

1962 — "Promoted" to the back page and full colour.

1968 — Joined by Gnasher.

1974 — First appearance on front and back covers.

1976 — Dennis fan club launched. It now has over a million members.

1977 — Gnasher is given his own page.

1979 — Dennis welcomes a pig named Rasher.

1984 — Rasher is given his own page.

1988 — BEANO'S 50th birthday. Dennis goods appear in the shops.

1990 — Dennis stars in his own TV show on The Children's Channel.

1991 — Dennis celebrates his 40th birthday.

OH, NO!

HIPPOPOTAMUS

ZOO

WAIT TILL
YOUR COLD
BETTE

ACHO

CHOO

...OTAMUS